They told me to write about the things that I know, so that is what I have done. In this book, I celebrate and reflect upon my own experiences and the people and places intimately connected to this lifelong voyage of discovery. Because I also came across pure imagination on the way, there may be some pieces of work where, however hard you try, you will recognise no person, living or departed, nor place identifiable on a satnav. However there will probably be elements that, should we be acquainted, will remind you of me.

I would like to dedicate the book to my husband Sean, who has encouraged and supported my work and laughed at the jokes.

My thanks also to Philip Bell for putting it all together so patiently and to Shaun Cuff for his fine interpretation of my mermaid.

G000088352

First published by Beachy Books in 2019
www.beachybooks.com

ISBN: 978-1-9997283-1-1

Set in Palatino

The Mermaid is Unimpressed

Sandy Kealty

BEACHY BOOKS

Contents

I moved to the Isle of Wight from Kent in 2003; a new home, a new marriage, a new start. What an adventure! And how romantic to take a ferry to go to Debenhams or John Lewis, take in a concert or visit a friend!

The Mermaid is Unimpressed

The day I saw a mermaid in the Solent
was a day like any other when very little happens.
I had passed the time by staring
at the gooseberry-jelly water
with its peaks of brownish foam,
drinking coffee; more expensive
than it would have been at home.

The day I saw my mermaid through the window,
I noticed that the ferry now
has wooden knives and forks;
it made me smile.

Oh why, I thought, had I not planned
and brought my own utensils,
folding mug or thermos,
a napkin from my linen drawer,
a statement made with style!

My mermaid floated idly, only just below the surface,
hair spread out like old unravelled rope.
She grinned with little pointy teeth,
her eyes as old as pebbles,
then, to my surprise and awe,
she spoke.

"How clever are your changes
and your wooden sticks for stirring,
but don't you think it's all a bit too late?
Do you really need to wander
round the shops for hours and hours?
Your greed for frocks is something
to which I can't relate."

She wasn't wearing much,
my mermaid in the Solent,
just the right amount for mermaids,
nothing gaudy, nothing gay.

She rose up on her fishy tail.
She glared and then began to wail,
"And while you fill your bags with stuff,
although you have more than enough
to sink a ship (oh happy, happy thought),
I'm choking here on diesel
and I know that soon the seas'll
be impossible to live in, so your scientists report."

She shook her head, my mermaid,
spat, swore, grimaced,
then slowly swam away.

When I told them of my mermaid, back on the Isle of Wight,
they stated very firmly that my brain's not working right.
No one else has seen a mermaid. No one else is likely to.
They fixed me with that look that says,
"My dear, there's something wrong with you."
They fixed me with that look that says,
"I'm glad it's you not me."
Then they put me in this room, in dismal, darkening gloom
and I rather think they've thrown away the key.

I retired not long after I arrived here. The Island's network of footpaths beckoned and I got me a map. Recently I have found that walking poles provide support and additional joie de vivre. I researched their history.

Nordic Walking

It's a Finnish thing.
For a hundred days of constant sun,
they canoodle and carouse,
as giddy as a Finn can be.

For a hundred days of constant sun,
the snow recedes and the skis are hung
in the shed, greased and ready
for the dark ahead.

They canoodle and carouse,
the muscles wither,
the waistlines grow,
then a Finn less sybaritic
cries, "Who needs snow!"

No giddiness here
as they persevere
on naked rock and soft green meadow.
Ski poles for summer!
Three lusty cheers for the fine fit Finns.

It's been around for eighty years.
I've taken the training,
I've purchased the gear.

Out on the sand in a brisk, bright breeze,
trousers rolled, not quite to my knees,
peach in my pocket.

Freed from the irk of limbs that don't work
and lungs that are bunged with silt.
On a roll with my poles, as the tide creeps in,
uplifted, enthused, though others are amused,
I'm off like a rocket.

When our winter comes,
I'll wear mittens with thumbs and a hat with a plait.
Oh, nothing can diminish walking in Finnish.

Unfortunately, there are days when enthusiasm wanes.

And the Living is Easy

Today will bring long hours of light, warm air and birdsong.
Rampant energy carouses in the vegetable patch,
eager beans race widdershins up sticks and canes,
bees exchange hot news around the lupins,
fecund roses sag and blow.

I will rise early, make the most of it,
walk briskly through the fields to forest edge and back,
climb overgrown, neglected stiles and slash at nettles.
Then breakfast; fruit, nuts, no decadent patisserie for me.

And then to work! Find brushes!
Wipe cobwebs from the tins of paint we bought last year.
The shed looks dowdy, still displaying grimy residue of winter.
The fences have a battered mien.
How splendid to restore
their Mediterranean sumptuousness!

That done, I may revive the water feature,
let rip the battle with convolvulus,
resume the slug wars,
and the slaughter of persistent aphids.

The temperature, meanwhile, is rising,
with pollen saturation keeping step.
I shift a tabby bundle from my lap.
She swipes my ankles as I stand.
The radio drones repeated tales of mayhem.

My glad resolve is done.
I think I'll just stay here,
by the window,
taking stock.
Perhaps I have a dose of melancholy.
It's known that sadness often blocks one's paths to righteousness.

Perhaps I have a dose of indolence.

In my childhood, summers were much more like hard work.

À la Recherche du Tent Perdu

In the long ago,
when phone calls cost four copper pennies,
and were not made without the smell of cigarettes and wee,
when slipper-slaps were hard and frequent,
recommended to good parents
to stop the young ones running free,
the proper thing to do each summer
was to herd us to the Morris Traveller,
with trailer following behind.
The camping season!
Such adventures!
Such broadening of the mind.

Our lists were made,
all necessaries packed in hefty biscuit tins,
(the grocers' sort, no cottages or portraits of the Queen),
each colour coded; green and yellow, grey, blue,
scarlet, orange; each a meaningful, remembered hue.

We would arrive at dusk in some far corner of a foreign field,
my brother having asked directions.
He, being very young, had not one word of French or German,
but Papa was quite convinced that characters are much improved
through learning by osmosis.

Then to the tins;
the green for pegs and mallets, bags of string,
the red for stoves, the grey for kettle, tea and mugs,
and so the camp would rise
and I would play my mouth organ, keeping spirits high,
whilst Mother found the cool box,
iced her swollen ankles,
and forgot, as usual, to complain.

Defying this sweet order was the mystery of the fruit bowl.
It had no place.
My brother wore it on his head from Dover to Firenze,
released from duty only when conversing with the natives.

Why am I now reminded of those happy days?
Sixty years have passed, but camping left its mark,
along with other little matters from the dark side.
My brother, having hoarded memories, artefacts and painted tins,
has finally been to see a counsellor.
He took the tins, consigned them to recycling.
He sent the mouth organ, now full of dust, to me.
He bought a caravan for weekends in the forest,
and hopefully moved on.

Cultural enlightenment was also available for the post-war child at school.

Worcester Grammar School for Girls, Summer Term

In the Hall for morning worship,
wriggling knees on parquet blocks,
homogenised in navy gym slips,
straggling ties and off-white socks.

Class of nineteen fifty seven,
slightly niffy in the heat,
not quite absorbed in thoughts of Heaven,
our earthly lives still long and sweet.

Batgowned mistresses, unmarried,
remaindered by the two world wars,
wise and subtle, mad and arid,
some despised and some adored.

Arching windows lit our mystery,
roses flourished in the quad.
Our worlds were split by time and history,
as we dreamed and sang of God.

We soon outgrew their wise restrictions,
"Don't talk to boys!" and "Wear your hat!"
Our dreaming led to strong convictions
that we knew far more than that.

"Be still and know" was our school motto,
begging to be turned around.
Lie still, find out, but first get blotto.
Fling your blanket on the ground.

Now it's many decades later,
did it all, the whole damned show.
It's closed and gone, my alma mater;
doesn't feel that long ago.

I dress this one with the information that my father would not allow me to have a bike, for fear that I might accidentally run into a sheep or, worse still, become chippy and unmanageable.

My New Bike

My new bike will be the colour of flaming sunset,
of clouds shaped like wolves and witches,
of flat sea retreating over green-gold mud.

My new bike will have thirty gears, including reverse.
I'll understand them all and change them flawlessly,
because I speak the language.
We will be one, each with the other.

My new bike will be just so high.
My feet will reach the ground,
but they will only need to
at the end and the beginning.

My new bike will have a capacious basket
for carrying ET and similar exotics,
but it will not slow us down,
as we speed across the moon in a perfect arc,
whooping triumphantly through the long nights of stars.

My new bike will have a comfortable saddle,
a perfect fit without appearing ungainly,
no fear of weariness or chafing,
as we explore the wonders of the world,
and, after cake at Freshwater, the universe.

My new bike will be superlight,
for otherwise I would find portage
across slippery, perfidious stones
above mighty cataracts,
a trifle onerous
and that just would not do.

My new bike will be tough.
It will never be trampled by the rhinoceroses
that lurk through life.
It will bounce off obstacles it cannot avoid,
and neither of us will require radical repair, ever.

My new bike will gleam and flash.
A great thrumming song will emanate from its spokes
and I will sing in magnificent harmony.
The noise will be stupendous,
especially at meal times and Sunday mornings,
and when The News is on.

My new bike will have a thermal force field,
so I can wear whatever I please,
including scraps of tight black leather and chains and armbracelets.
I will be Sandra, Warrior Princess, with no flabby bits,
for cycling is excellent exercise.

My new bike is in the shed and soon I'll learn to ride it,
for now that Daddy's safely dead, there is no need to hide it.

There were good bits of course, but I wrote this one saddened by proliferating news, that some of our childhood heroes were not all they were cracked up to be.

History Lesson

We used to pick bluebells;
armfuls, drooling viscous sap
as we trailed them home,
past the pig farm and the gas works,
our refreckled noses exalting
in a haze of blue perfume.

We used to disappear all day;
water bottle borrowed from Corona,
jam sandwich and a filched potato,
over the Common to wave at trains,
shout, light fires,
create hierarchies,
adopt secret names and rituals.
Sometimes we tied my little brother up.
He said he liked it.

We used to throw stones at conker trees,
bake, skewer, string the loot,
compete with furious concentration,
no gloves, no goggles.
The victories warmed our pride.
The bruises faded.

We used to walk to school knee-deep in snow
when buses could not run
and we could.
Drank frostbit milk at play time,
sucking plugs of ice like summer lollies,
made slides,
fell over,
broke bones,
scratched chilblains.

They're trying to tell me now this life was all delusion,
wrong, skewed, grimed in wickedness and lust.
Perhaps I'll disappear over the Common,
before they turn the scent of bluebells into dust.

This vaguely metaphorical poem is for two voices, Authority and Me. Old habits die hard.

Roaming Rites

In the green light,
I smell leaf mould,
dry now, friable,
home to small things.
I will examine them.

You must not walk willy-nilly alone in the woods.
You must join an organised tour on a Sunday.
It isn't safe without a guide.
Be advised,
there are no bears,
nor wolves,
but there are other things,
and we know best.

I watch the centipedes
and the militant ants
skittering through the litter.
Nearby, the last bear
smiles indulgently.

You must observe the painted notice.
There is a bye-law,
and discussions have been taking place on Facebook.
Woods are perilous!
We can assure,
there are no scabrous bats,
nor lynx, nor puma, wild of paw,
but there are dangers that are quite beyond your ken.

I look up through the dizzy trees.
A striped tail hangs.
A fanged, bewhiskered face looks back.
We nod.
It's not yet time for pipistrelles.

The reality of the past does have a habit of catching up with one. This is what happened when my mother and I cleared the last mountain of my father's leavings. We had already filled several skips with items that could have come in useful. They never did.

Moving On

You may have heard it rapturously reported,
the great collection has at last been sorted.
My father's cupboard and the boxes labelled "later"
emptied of their contents by his wife and daughter.
Emptied of their power, emptied of their life,
emptied of their damned demands on daughter and on wife.

Proper ceremony was observed.
Her pain, my rage, our mutual bewilderment,
needed more than swift and sensible decisions.
We each sought out our ways to best
lay more than half a century to rest.
The provenance of each discovery
was given voice, considered, put in order.

What was there?
Oh, everything and nothing.
Inventions, thieves of time and skill,
intentions, mostly unfulfilled,
things eclectic, things electric, eccentricities.
Mystery; "I think he made it for extracting tent pegs."
History; a box of stuff from when he was a spy,
a diplomatic pass from Bucharest,
mementos from the Balkans.
An illustration might shed light
upon the sheer dimensions of our plight.

My Dad used to follow the postie around.
He'd stare intently at the ground,
crowing with elation when he found
discarded rubber bands, so thick and strong,
often damp and smelly, but exceptionally long.

There they were, in a biscuit tin,
perished, stuck together, begging for the bin.

A small cardboard box was nearly our undoing,
tarnished silver horseshoes, ancient icing,
an artificial flower, long dead.

But they too were discarded.
For we agreed that all these things
were best remembered in one's head.
There they could wear the freshness of their youth,
not layered dust, which interferes with truth.

Perhaps our lack of cohesion as a family was a communication problem. That sort of thing can become insurmountable.

Living in Each Other's Pockets

You keep your pockets tucked away somewhere.
And mine; I can't remember when I saw them last.
No chance of our resuming mutual residence
along with peppermints and interesting fluff.

You bring me tea at half past seven,
we meet again for breakfast at half eight,
discuss the day's necessities,
admire the cat,
tread on eggshells.
Then I to potter in my shed,
and you to cricket on the television.

The days pile high,
the time-born barriers solidify.
Perhaps if we could clamber to the summit,
we might glimpse the country we've vacated,
recognise the pathways,
the waymarkers.

But it's a perilous climb,
and we are tired and ache in every bone.
The map, in any case, is writ by idiots.
We would not understand its language.

I guess our pockets should have been
more spacious, deeper,
more accommodating,
displayed in honest view,
accessible, like keepsakes
on the mantelpiece.

Indeed, such failings could have fatal consequences.

Vanishing Cream

The first layer she shed was thin as the skin on water.
She caught it for a fraction of a second,
but the action fragmented it, dissipated it to air.

She hadn't taken note of what her husband had been saying
when she felt this microscopic flaying.
Was it the joke about the moisturiser
that purported to be time-delaying?
She used it every night, but still the weeks flew by.

She found herself increasingly rubbed up the wrong way.
Her inner self abraded,
whilst skin attenuating on its frame of bones continued;
masqueraded as the wife at home, cooked, shopped, cleaned
and answered telephones.

He noticed she was quieter, but that was no great disadvantage.
Match of the Day would not be interrupted,
less irritating natter at the table.
If there were something wrong, surely she would say.
He blamed her hormones.
She began to feel light-headed,
tried to ignore the growing emptiness,
kept her feet upon the ground.

A crisis was inevitable.
At eight, a knock upon the door, a policeman, looking grim.
"There's been an incident," he said, "D'you mind if I come in?"

She'd been in Tesco's, dithering, unable now to make decisions.
A fast young sprig came barging by,
deploying neither brain, nor ear, nor eye;
a mistimed step, an accidental move, a terrible collision.

A brief hiatus, then a yell of disbelief, disgust;
where once she stood, a pile of dust.
Her fragile crust had been too thin,
too tightly stretched to ride the impact,
its bony cage made parched and brittle,
as day by day and little by little,
the good moist centre of her self had withered.

Homily.
If you allow the slights of others to diminish
your own sweet substance,
this could be how you will finish.

I realise that dust features strongly in my work, as do beans. I wonder if I yet have time to find out why. However, here we are commenting on the scientific principle that matter changes but does not disappear. We are all made of the dust of our ancestors. I am so pleased that mine included the Scattergoods, though the bishop is also quite a coup.

Mattermorphosis

So much dust;
a bishop, a lady's maid,
a soubrette, the bizarre Scattergoods.
One false step.
one cataclysmic breath,
and back they float
into the dust pool.

So much dust,
flaked from former selves.
In me, the girl who would not eat spring onions,
the girl who would not speak,
the girl who would not stop speaking,
the meadow larker,
the bleak face at the window.

So much dust.
No wonder that I am grown large.
I will have to make me a new coat.
I will need to get me a sturdy length of cloth,
and we can wrap ourselves,
motes without motion,
biding our time in its ample folds.

There was a time in later life when I was left alone and needed cheerfulness. Imaginary friends, I discovered, are not just for nippers.

Fantasia

Lars and Sven, those excellent men,
I'll never invent your like again.
Lars, dark and stocky, and Sven, tall and blonde,
oh, why did you leave me?
What made you abscond?

Dear Sven, you were attentive on bad hair days.
Enfolding me in sweet smiles, lying praise,
and, when the sunsets were particularly exquisite,
when I was alone on my balcony made for two,
drinking fine wine from a fine glass,
or gin,
I would, with an ironic grin,
raise a toast to you, my friend.
When asked who I would take to the barbecue,
who would squire me to the ball,
I'd turn to you,
and ride out all the nods, the badly hidden sneers.

I wasn't very good at being a widow.
My tangible choices all had feet of clay
and baggage heaped in vast left luggage halls.
So, one by one, I blew them all away.
I conjured you to share the joke,
and gave you all the makings of a proper bloke.

Then came the time when Maude,
(whose name's been changed to shield me from her ire)
found herself adrift a whole long summer. Dire it was.
Concerned, I made up your best mate,
informed my friend she had a date,
a foursome with myself and Sven and Lars.

She fell upon my wild invention,
which truly wasn't my intention,
for it lost the lightly mocking touch
that made it such a joy.
But I went on, proprietorial blindness
insisting it was just a simple act of kindness.
Caught up, I was, in that initial philanthropic rush.
Alas, she swiftly turned my bonny boys to mush.

First they took to quiet conversations in private nooks,
then came melancholy looks, then nervous silences,
so different from our previous noisy sport.
They took up squash and conversational Flemish,
and still I didn't recognise the blemish
that threatened to engulf our sweet quartet.

You cannot dance when eggshells strew the floor beneath.
You cannot sing when every inhalation is a wholly envied breath.
And there it was, the death of Lars and Sven.

She, to assuage her guilt, insisted they had run away
to a hippy men's camp, hugging trees,
but, to my considerable unease,
I knew this was not so.
Deep down, I knew I'd never see the boys again,
dear Lars and even dearer Sven.
About this time, Maude met a man of flesh,
and, while their friendship was still fresh,
persuaded him to redesign her garden.
I think, and look for no one's pardon,
my boys are buried there beneath the lawn,
and so, bereft, I'm left alone to mourn.

The moral of this tale is plain.
However loud her groans of pain,
there are some rare occasions when
you should not share your sweeties with a friend.

And life did get better – much better. I tell people that this poem was inspired by a sign on the balcony at Quay Arts on a particularly lovely summer's day. It sort of was, but it is a little cheeky. I like the shape of it, don't you?

Signs and Portents

DANGER
DEEP
WATER

stark black
on clamorous yellow,
obscured
by summer-scented rosemary.

I focus on
the flowering branches,
a-bustle with bees.

I focus on
the flash and giggle of sunlight on the river,
forget that rosemary is for remembrance,
agree to meet again next Saturday
at my place,
offer to cook.

I add a mental note
to hoover,
dust,
and change the sheets.

A stepdaughter was added to the mix. Eventually that
worked quite well.

Off the Bedroom Wall

She's deep in thought, bed-changing paused,
with just the awkward corner of the bottom sheet untucked,
duvet cover spread out on the floor, ready for confrontation.

She's twenty one now.
I expect a conversation about fabric softener,
how sheets are so much more themselves when dried outdoors,
how right I am to insist on cotton,
even though it is a confounded nuisance
and needs ironing.

Her stance changes.
She raises her arms,
assumes a boxer's guard,
claws extended,
growls,
tears at the sheet with her foreshortened limbs,
tramples the duvet,
roars.
I can see her saurian tail
and many, many teeth.

"Wouldn't it," she says, with a terrifying grin,
"be a total bummer to be T Rex.
You'd never get the sheet tucked in."

I have to agree,
and we conclude
it's probably the reason why
he is so dangerous.

My new spouse is a sporting type, who gets quite excited
when he marmalises a younger man. That sort of thing does
take its toll.

Squashing the Opposition

Oh, see the crowds of cheering trippers.
They've come to see him whipping nippers!

The competitive edge
is maintained by ibuprofen
and a soak
in hot water
for an hour
or two,
plus visits to the osteopath
for massage
and noisy manipulation,
which keeps the knees
working.

Prepare his tea with bread and kippers,
for he is home from whipping nippers.

When he returns,
damp, flushed,
and looking chipper,
having out-thought,
outwitted,
outranked
today's hopeful,
I know that this defines his time
and how he needs to spend it.

For Einstein, sums; for Cousteau, flippers;
for him it must be whipping nippers.

Whilst I spend my time nurturing my protected Isle of Wight garden. I may have mentioned beans in a previous poem. Where would we be without them!

Gardening Notes From a Place of Safety

My first bean was
the subject of profound rejoicing.
Vigorous, determined,
the green of new-made things,
its head so lizard-like,
I called it Beanosaurus Rex.

A second followed,
a third, a fourth.
Fifth and sixth were laggardly;
and then no more.
The grapevine said
that beans are difficult this year.

I raised the matter
with a friend, who has a quandary
of a different sort;
unexpected beans,
rampaging on a wall he'd quite forgotten;
no provenance and wildness in their gaze.

A mutant strain,
carried over on the tide?
A most diverting thought and I am tempted,
but then consider giants,
tales of triffids,
concluding that discretion,
and a further sowing of my standard seed,
would be the better course.

Though my innate tendency to show off does blossom
occasionally.

A Trichological Treat

I wish I had a tower of hair
that I could stick some stuff in,
like butterflies and small pork pies,
to make you gasp and rub your eyes,
and jump around with mad surprise.
Though if I want the world to stare,
to shout out, "Look! Look over there!"
I'd top it with a seagull and a flower,
some tomatoes,
and a puffin.

And I do still sing, though am very aware that I should not wear out my welcome. This poem is for two voices. It might be fun to ham them up a bit ... I do.

The Fat Lady Considers Her Position

My arpeggios are lacking in lustre,
my pitch is just short of correct,
my acciaccatura
is without the bravura
my public has come to expect.
Is it time, my dear?

Yes, I fear, my dear,
that it's time for the end of the pier,
my dear.

No, I won't get all cranky and flustered,
though I'll sigh a quiet sigh of regret,
for my décolleté
simply gets in the way
when I try just a small pirouette.
Is it time, my dear?

Yes, I fear, my dear,
that it's time for the end of the pier,
my dear.

I know I can't quite cut the mustard,
though I'm far from entirely wrecked,
with a stiff G and T,
I still sound like me,
but it's not a long lasting effect.
Is it time, my dear?

You're sublime, my dear,
yet I fear, my dear,
it's time for the end
(and I speak as a friend)
it's time for the end of the pier.

You can still have some sort of career,
and the ocean's attractively near.
It's only for part of the year,
and nobody's going to sneer,
a tradition as British as beer
is the pier,
my dear.

Though a meek and retiring presentation is not always sensible. This is what happened when I was early for a meeting of assorted creatives at Dimbola Lodge and the reason for my presence was not immediately obvious.

Conversation at Dimbola

A beret, a feather,
lace-up boots in purple leather
from Anello and Davide;
a whiff of weed.

A toque, a cloak,
a desire to provoke,
lavish loops of lapis beads;
unreasonable needs.

A faraway gaze,
a tendency to graze
on tiny bits of cheese;
such things as these?

"You don't look like a poet,"
says our hostess with a smile,
masking her discomfort and distress.
Not poetic, me?
A frisson of raw panic,
I have a folder with me,
but I'm very quietly dressed.

A little early, drinking tea,
prosaic to the core,
(absinthe only on the menu
Fridays, after four).

It seems that I've mislaid my context.
Does my appearance now dictate
my place amongst those choosing to create?

Think, gentle reader, what this means,
resign yourself to growing beans,
design yourself for knitting socks;
the clocks move on.

However hard one tries, life does not always go smoothly.

Trousers

Today I put my trousers on the wrong way round;
not the wrong trousers, mark you,
just the right ones, incorrectly donned.
Sartorial senility, I suppose.
Soon it will be ill-matched hose,
topmost button fixed in thirdmost hole,
slippers in the snow.

Please may I ask that you inspect my turnout daily
to protect my reputation.
It would be nice to know that, once a day,
you see me as I am,
and then as I would wish to be.
It would be nice to know that, once a day,
you see me.

Occasionally these days, I become irascible. There are perfectly good reasons why.

On Learning About the Changes at Sainsbury's, Where I Have Shopped for Over Fifty Years. Other Retailers are Also Lined Up for Comment.

I do not want to join your family,
rate in stars the pants I bought on Amazon for my mother,
applaud the swift delivery.

Don't ask me how the concert was for me,
infantilise me with your smiley faces,
coax me to download apps because they're new and shiny.
I am not nine years old.
That was a lifetime ago,
before we started using plastic packaging.

Don't slot me into your algorithms.
How long before you seek to judge me
by the company I keep,
the cheese I buy,
which is, as I am sure you know,
the same each week,
as is the bread, the tea, the cat food?

This is the final straw.
I will go dark,
cut up my Nectar card
and shop with cash at Lidls,
with no reward,
but noticeably lower prices.

There have been setbacks; knees, hips and boomsidaisy, no less, but I find there is usually something to look forward to.

Hobble-dee, Hobble-dee and Down Into the Ditch

Just when I think it's safe
to dip a tentative toe in the water,
the orchestra starts up,
a full-tilt, four note figure,
carrying an unmistakeable message.
Swift exit.
Back up the beach.
Enrobe in comforting towels.
The inscription is irrelevant,
but panic is not indicated at this stage.
Ponder, if you must, upon the risks
encountered by cellists on soft sand,
and wonder how they arrive so serendipitously
in the nick of time.

Just when I think it's right
to stride out across the winter fields,
regaining fitness and the joy of breathing,
who should come prancing into camera but Gene Kelly,
with concomitant rainstorm.
How did he know my latitude,
my longitude, my longing?
A mystery,
but I will take cover.

Just when I think my altered plans
are quite the bitter end, the final straw,
a row too tough to hoe,
the sun comes out and shines on winter pansies,
first hints of rhubarb, a scattering of budding daffs.
So I will persevere,
give full attention to my exercises,
as instructed;
look to the future.

One's equilibrium can be restored by tangible and useful things and the memories they evoke.

My Grandmother's Hat

In leopard skin,
fake fur from 1959,
or thereabouts,
invented by her dancing brain,
constructed by her competent hands,
a triumph of a hat.

She wore it to choir practice
and on windy seafront walks,
where she watched birds and boats
and fellow promenaders.

In 1963 she added cherries,
and wore it in the orchard to confuse the wasps.
During winter '64, she wore it to bed,
it was so cold,
but, conscious of propriety,
she first removed
her matching scarlet lipstick.

Now that her bright soul has left the stage,
I have the hat.

I wear it to choir practice
and on windy seafront walks,
where I watch birds and boats,
and fellow promenaders.
I have replaced the cherries with more cherries.
I wear it at poetry readings to amuse the audience.
Last winter I wore it in the house,
it was so cold.

I would like to wear it when I have
no further use for lipstick.
It would not suit my brother's daughters,
and I think its solace
would be lost on them.

My grandmother did not stop at hats. She was a skilled tailor and needlewoman who kept us all turned out spic and span when there was little to be had and that was rationed. Her sewing room was heaven.

From My Ration Book

The post-war blues are all but done.
No more conjuring the New Look from the old,
with all the good bits reconfigured into this and that,
a summer dress, a winter coat, a hat.
No more guarding points and doing as we're told,
now we can buy without restriction.

In my grandma's attic, a thunder of activity,
speeding up the seams, setting sleeves just so,
fiddling with facings, binding blasted buttonholes,
getting it all done before the van has to go.

Marks and Spencer's outwork, bringing her prosperity,
giving solid substance to post-privation dreams,
notching up her income, nudging out frugality,
with treadle to the metal, stacking up the means
to buy a new Ford Anglia, first motor in the family.
She took it round the pretty routes to breathe in country scenes.

Such work is now outsourced and gone.
We gobble up this season's fancy without thought.
And yet I cannot pass an Oxfam by
without a glance for buried treasure.
Under my bed there lies my hedge against inflation;
fabrics which, from time to time,
I touch and ponder, and then fold away.

There is such pleasure in the lace my grandma wore,
the little piece of silk I've had since I was ten,
a soft brown velvet dress, discovered at a jumble sale,
too small and out of date to wear again,
the yards and metres of more humble stuff,
put by and waiting for my cutting table.

The sewing room and my good grandma
are both long departed, but the legacy remains.
I too can bind a buttonhole, set an awkward sleeve.
I too can seize upon the hour to relish every minute,
and find renewal in a breath of country air.
I too can reconfigure,
a skill that might be useful in the coming times.

I take my wicked stepmother duties seriously, and here I suggest the proper response at the end of a relationship where a desire to control becomes an issue. I too once suffered such tyranny. Can you believe it!

Off To Buy a Scarlet Frock

I will not be defined by limitations
that are yours alone.
I will not cover up my youth and strength
with dowdy cardigans,
unless the wind is tearing off the Bay,
and I am chilly.

Now you have gone,
I'll learn to please myself.
My wardrobe is my own affair.
It may not lead to Narnia,
but the possibilities
are utterly enchanting.

But there are some things that no amount of staunch resolve can cure. I have known too many people living with dementia. My mother in law has joined their ranks, which means, I guess, that we have too.

Mirror Mirror

They cover the mirrors,
because it's upsetting
to see yourself when
you don't know who you are.

They cover the mirrors,
because you might hide there
or tumble right through,
though you wouldn't get far.

But she wanted a mirror
for doing her lipstick,
so he bought a robust one
sealed tight in its frame.

She dismantled the mirror,
though her fingers are clumsy;
they don't work like they used to,
well nothing's the same.

She gave him the mirror,
wrapped up in a hanky,
for it carried her likeness
to remember her by.

Don't think he'll forget her.
When he looks in the mirror,
there's something familiar
in the shade of his eyes.

To cheer us up, another excursion to the woods. We must enjoy them while they are still there! More dust, but thankfully, no beans.

Changes

She loved the woods;
dazzle of sudden sunlight,
pneumatic layers
of nests and tunnelling bugs,
of fungus, leaf, decay
and seeds in hiding.

She loved the scent;
peppery in the dry of summer,
sulphurous when the ditches filled.
In April, ramsons, wild and pungent.
In May, the swagger of dancing bluebells,
giving way to bracken, dust and nettle.

She loved the sound;
swish, slide and sudden snapping underfoot,
rattle of ripening gorse pods,
howl of gale in winter branches,
whisper of its younger cousin through spring green,
chitter of birds.

Now she is grounded and the woods are gone,
their subtle pleasures many years away.
But she remembers, and is heartened,
dawdling with dogroses, just out for the day.

And finally, a celebration of the season of mists, a more modern view, more cautious. I will tell you about caution (and motorbikes and hip hop) in my next book.

The First Fog of Autumn

Molly said
she saw a critter in the mist,
fell of claw and draped in bloody tatters,
but she's a cat, and very old.
I do not trust her judgement.

Molly said
we ought to leave right now,
before the others come, they might be hungry,
but she's a cat and cats exaggerate.
I see no need to panic.

Molly said
"I told you so."
They came in force and we are under siege.
Resistance may be futile.